STYLE IT: TRENDS AND FADS

Hot Hair

by VIRGINIA LOH-HAGAN

45TH PARALLEL PRESS

Published in the United States of America by
Cherry Lake Publishing Group
Ann Arbor, Michigan
www.cherrylakepublishing.com

Reading Adviser: Beth Walker Gambro, MS, Ed., Reading Consultant, Yorkville, IL
Book Designer: Joseph Hatch

Photo Credits: © Yevgeniy Zateychuk/Shutterstock, cover; Harry Cooke/Pexels.com, 4;
The Earthy Jay/Pexels.com, 7; Rogier van der Weyden, Public domain, via Wikimedia
Commons, 8; Image courtesy of Sister Sky, 11; Smithsonian American Art Museum, Gift
of John Gellatly, 13; Office of the California Assembly, Public domain, via Wikimedia
Commons, 14; © Kristin Smith/Shutterstock, 16; © Aleksei Smyshliaev/iStock.com, 19;
© Angelica Pasquali/Shutterstock, 21; AJEONG_JM, CC BY 4.0 via Wikimedia Commons, 22;
© Mike Orlov/Shutterstock, 24; Abhishek Shekhawat/Pexels.com, 27; © LightField
Studios/Shutterstock, 28; Tima Miroshnichenko/Pexels.com, 31

Copyright © 2026 by Cherry Lake Publishing Group

All rights reserved. No part of this book may be reproduced or utilized in any form
or by any means without written permission from the publisher.

45th Parallel Press is an imprint of Cherry Lake Publishing Group.

Library of Congress Cataloging-in-Publication Data

Names: Loh-Hagan, Virginia author
Title: Hot hair / by Virginia Loh-Hagan.
Description: Ann Arbor, Michigan : 45th Parallel Press, [2025] | Series: Style it: Trends
    and fads | Audience: Grades 7-9 | Summary: "The newest hairstyles were hot way
    back when and they're still hot now! Take a look at the modern and historical trends
    and fads that have come and gone in the world of hair. Readers of these hi-lo books
    will be surprised by various trends and fads that will keep them guessing until the
    very end"— Provided by publisher.
Identifiers: LCCN 2025009360 | ISBN 9781668963814 (hardcover) | ISBN 9781668965139
    (paperback) | ISBN 9781668966747 (ebook) | ISBN 9781668968352 (pdf)
Subjects: LCSH: Hairstyles | Hairstyles—History—Juvenile literature. | Hairstyles—Social
    aspects—Juvenile literature. | Ornamental hairwork—Juvenile literature.
Classification: LCC GT2290 .L64 2025 | DDC 391.509—dc23/eng/20250428
LC record available at https://lccn.loc.gov/2025009360

Cherry Lake Publishing Group would like to acknowledge the work of the Partnership
for 21st Century Learning, a Network of Battelle for Kids. Please visit Battelle for Kids
online for more information.

Note from publisher: Websites change regularly, and their future contents are outside
of our control. Supervise children when conducting any recommended online searches
for extended learning opportunities.

Printed in the United States of America

**Dr. Virginia Loh-Hagan is an author and educator. She is currently the Executive
Director for Asian American Native Hawaiian Pacific Islander Affairs at San Diego
State University and the Co-Executive Director of The Asian American Education
Project. She lives in San Diego with her very tall husband and very naughty dogs.**

TABLE of CONTENTS

INTRODUCTION 5

CHAPTER 1: **Big Foreheads** 9

CHAPTER 2: **Japanese Topknots** 10

CHAPTER 3: **Rat's Nest** 12

CHAPTER 4: **Jazz Age Hair** 15

CHAPTER 5: **Beehives** 17

CHAPTER 6: **Liberty Spikes** 18

CHAPTER 7: **Gumby Haircut** 20

CHAPTER 8: **Bowl Cuts** 23

CHAPTER 9: **Glitter Hair**........................ 25

CHAPTER 10: **Modern Mullets** 26

DO YOUR PART! 29

GLOSSARY.. 32

LEARN MORE 32

INDEX.. 32

There are always new hair trends!
Which ones have you seen lately?

INTRODUCTION

Everybody has style. Some people have more style than others. They stand out. They use **fashion** to express themselves. Fashion is about how people want to look. It's about how people dress. It includes clothes, shoes, hats, and jewelry. It also includes hairstyles and makeup.

Fashion changes across cultures. It changes over time. There are many fashion **trends**. Trends are fads. They're patterns of change. They reflect what's popular at a certain time. Many people copy popular looks. They copy famous people. They get inspired. They want to be cool. They want to be in style.

Some trends last a long time. Other trends are short. All trends make history.

Hair is one of the first things people notice about other people. It's on top of your head. It frames your face.

People like to style their hair. They cut their hair. They arrange their hair. They decorate their hair. They dye their hair. They shave off their hair. They have fake hair. They have fun with their hair.

Hairstyles can change how people look. They add beauty. They add personality. They signal one's role in society. They play a key role in fashion.

Some hairstyles are big. Some are elegant. Some are simple. There have been a lot of hairstyle trends. This book features some of the fun ones!

Hairstyles can be connected to culture. They can hold deep cultural meanings.

This Rogier van der Weyden painting, *Portrait of a Lady*, was painted around 1460.

CHAPTER

One

Big Foreheads

Big foreheads were trendy in 15th-century Europe. Women spent hours getting this look. They plucked hairs from their hairlines. They pulled their hairlines back several inches. They plucked hair from their temples. They plucked hair from their necks. They also plucked their eyebrows to a fine line. This took hours. It was painful. Some women shaved their hairlines instead.

The ideal look would be as smooth as a baby's head. A high forehead was a sign of beauty. It was also a sign of a high class. It also signaled being smart. People thought big foreheads meant big brains!

Women also wore headpieces. These pieces pulled their hair back. They made their foreheads look even larger.

CHAPTER
TWO

Japanese Topknots

Chonmage is a Japanese topknot hairstyle. It was worn by men. It was worn by **samurai**. Samurai were highly trained warriors.

Chonmage was most popular in the Edo period. The Edo period took place from 1603 to 1868.

The top of the head was shaved. The remaining hair was oiled and waxed. Then it was tied into a small tail. The tail was folded onto the top of the head.

Samurai had to wear heavy helmets. This trapped heat. Shaving their heads had a purpose. It kept the head cool in battle. And chonmage was more than just helpful. It was also a proud symbol. It showed honor, pride, and loyalty.

FASHION-FORWARD PIONEER

People have different hair types. Marina TurningRobe and Monica Simeon know this. They're sisters. They're Native Americans. They grew up on the Spokane Indian Reservation. They're in business together. In 1999, they started Sister Sky. Sister Sky sells hair care products. They also sell soaps and lotions. Their products are designed for mixed texture hair. Their mission is to "provide inclusive and effective hair care products that empower individuals with diverse hair to embrace their natural beauty with confidence." They use native herbs. Their products are **vegan**. This means no animals were used. They're changing the beauty business. They're focusing on culture. Simeon said, "Our concept of wellness comes from our cultural values."

First and second generations of this Indigenous, woman-and-family-owned company pose together. *Left to right:* Marina TurningRobe, Stephanie TurningRobe, Sophia TurningRobe, and Monica Simeon

CHAPTER
THREE

Rat's Nest

Marie Antoinette was the last queen of France. She ruled from 1774 to 1793. She was a huge influencer. She popularized the **pouf**. This was a hairstyle in which hair was piled up in rolled puffs. She wore big, tall wigs. They were styled into poufs.

These wigs had themes. They were showy. They had many objects. They used wire to hold everything in place. Everything was bonded together with **lard**. Lard is animal fat. It smelled. It attracted rats. Rats made their homes in these wigs. That's why some people today call messy hair a rat's nest.

Women wore these wigs for a week or two. They slept with several pillows to stay upright. They had to duck when walking through doors.

Marie Antoinette, Queen of France, wearing one of her infamous wigs

FASHION REBEL: TRENDSETTER

Holly J. Mitchell wears locs. She is a Black American politician. She was a California state senator from 2013 to 2020. In 2019, she introduced the CROWN Act. CROWN stands for Creating a Respectful and Open Workplace for Natural Hair. This act was signed into law. It was the first law to ban hair bias in workplaces and schools. It protected natural hair. It protected styles like locs, braids, and twists. These hairstyles differed from White standards of beauty. Some people were punished. A sixth grader was suspended for wearing braids. A high schooler was forced to cut his dreadlocks. Mitchell's act protected Black hairstyles. She set a trend. Other states and cities followed.

CHAPTER

FOUR

Jazz Age Hair

The 1920s in the United States was known as the Jazz Age. It was a time of change. Women moved away from long hair.

At first, hair was just pulled up. Teenage girls wore flat buns around their ears. These buns looked like earphones. This hairstyle was also called "**cootie** garages." Cooties are another name for lice. The buns hid lice.

Soon, a new style took over. Women cut off their long hair. **Bobbed** haircuts were in. Hair was cut short and straight. It was about chin-length. Women rebelled against gender roles. They wanted more freedom. Bobbed hair was bold.

The beehive was a go-to style for many women in the 1960s.

CHAPTER

five

Beehives

In the 1960s, big hair was back. Women would pile up their long hair. They made a cone shape. The cone leaned back. This hairstyle looked like a beehive. It had lots of volume. It was highly styled. Hair had to be teased with a comb.

The beehive is also known as the B-52. A B-52 is a **bomber**. Bombers are planes that drop bombs.

Hairstylist Margaret Vinci Heldt created the beehive. Heldt entered a contest. She based the hairstyle on a small black hat. She was inspired by a model wearing a bee hatpin.

CHAPTER

Liberty Spikes

Liberty spikes trended in the 1970s. The name was inspired by the Statue of Liberty's crown. Hair was grown long. People formed it into tall spikes. Spikes could be longer than 1 foot (0.3 meters). Some people dyed the spikes different colors.

British **punk** popularized this look. Punk is a youth movement. Punk rock music is fast and hard. It's the opposite of folk and disco music. Hippies and disco fans had long, smooth hairstyles. Punk fans preferred messy, spiky hairstyles.

Liberty spikes can last for a few days. They require lots of gel and hairspray.

People use products to get their liberty spikes to stand up straight. Beeswax, gel, and even glue can make this style stick.

CHAPTER

seven

Gumby Haircut

Gumby is a cartoon character from the 1950s. He was revived in the 1980s. He is green. He is shaped like a blocky human. He is made of clay. His head is slanted.

The Gumby haircut was popular in the 1980s and 1990s. It has a flat top. It's slightly slanted. It has sharp edges. It has closely shaved sides and back.

The cut was part of rap culture. It was mainly worn by Black American men. Hip-hop artists made it popular. The Gumby haircut was also part of the new jack swing movement. New jack swing blends rap, pop, jazz, funk, and rhythm and blues. This haircut is still popular with some people today.

DIY FASHION FUN

ADD SOME FLAIR TO YOUR HAIR. MAKE YOUR OWN HAIR DECORATIONS. HERE ARE SOME IDEAS:

» Make your own scrunchies. Scrunchies are fabric-covered hair ties. They were popular in the 1980s and 1990s. Today, they're back in style.

» Tie ribbons to your ponytails. Save ribbons when unwrapping gifts. Make a bow or leave hanging. This is a classic look. It has been around for years. Today, ribbons in hair offer a "balletcore" look.

» Weave flowers into your braids. This is part of a "cottagecore" style. This look is simple and pretty. It reminds people of being in the country.

CHAPTER

EIGHT

Bowl Cuts

Bowl cuts are shaped like an upside-down bowl. The hair is cut to the same length all around the head. The sides and back are cut short. The top is long. It's a clean, neat look.

This hairstyle is often seen on young kids. It's been around a while. It was commonly worn by monks in 500 to 1500. In the 1960s, the Beatles popularized this look. The Beatles were a famous British rock band.

Today, South Korean boy bands are trending bowl cuts. Since the 1990s, Korean pop music has been all the rage. K-pop artists are superstars. Many male K-pop artists have bowl cuts. These cuts are youthful. They're playful.

Some members of the K-pop group BTS have bowl cuts.

Today, people use big and colorful glitter.
They want to make sure it doesn't look like dandruff.

CHAPTER

nine

Glitter Hair

People have always added shimmer to their hair. Ancient Romans used gold dust. In the 1980s, people used glitter hair sprays. In the 2000s, people added **tinsel** to their hair. Tinsel is thin, shiny strips of paper or plastic. Tinsel is woven into hair. It can be clipped in. This trend is called "fairy hair."

In the 2020s, sparkly strands are back. Fairy hair is still popular. Glitter is applied directly to hair. This can be done with sprays or gels. It can also be done by mixing glitter with hairspray.

There are different ways to add glitter. One style is glitter roots. Glitter roots are popular at music festivals. Glitter is just added to the roots. Or glitter can be sprinkled on a center part.

CHAPTER

Ten

Modern Mullets

"Business in the front. Party in the back." Mullets are cut short on the sides and top. Hair is left long in the back. It was a popular 1970s and 1980s men's haircut.

2020 was called "the year of the mullet." This was due to the COVID-19 lockdown and closed hair salons. Men kept a business look up front for video calls.

Modern mullets have a cleaner look. Sides are kept short. But the top and back hair are long. Cuts can be changed to suit one's style. They can be faded. They can be layered. Options are endless.

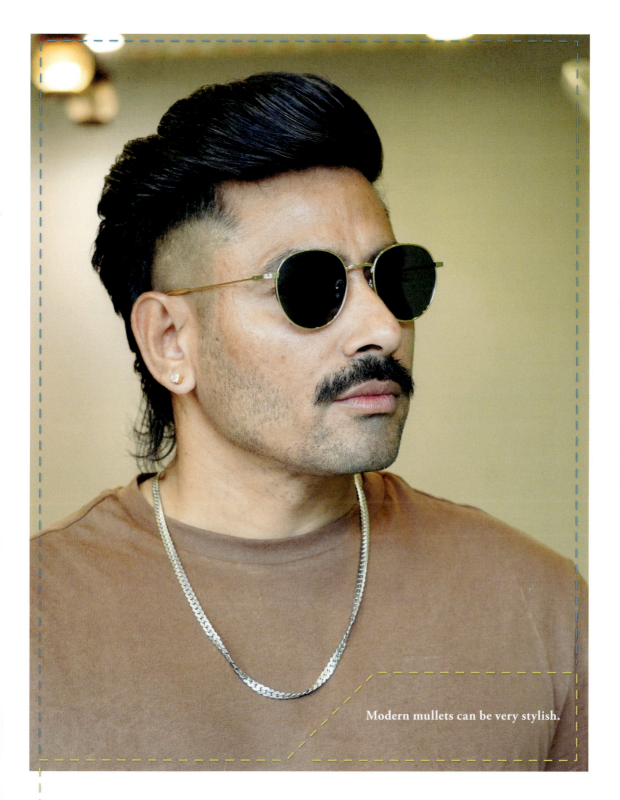

Modern mullets can be very stylish.

Many people prefer hair products that aren't made using animals.

DO YOUR PART!

It's always fashionable to stand up for what's right. Fashion can be more than just about looks. It can be used to fight for causes. Be a fashion **activist**. Activists fight for change. They want a better world. Here are some ways to make a difference:

- Use **cruelty-free** hair products. Hair products include shampoo, gel, and hairspray. Many products are tested on animals. Cruelty-free means no animals were harmed. Protect animals while still having great hair.

- Use vegan hair products. Some products might contain honey or milk. Honey comes from bees. Milk comes from cows. Vegan products use only plants.

- Donate your hair. Donated hair should be 8 to 12 inches (20.3 to 30.5 centimeters) long. Some people have hair loss. They may be sick. They need wigs. Grow your hair long. Get it cut. Give it to groups who make wigs. This helps people feel better. Plus, there are many cute short hairstyles. And hair grows back!

- Recycle hair. Hair can be used for many things. It can help plants grow. It can clean up oil spills. It can be made into mats to cover storm drains. It can be used as stuffing. Save your hair. Help the environment.

Remember, every little bit counts. Kindness matters. You can look good and feel great!

FIGHTING FOR JUSTICE

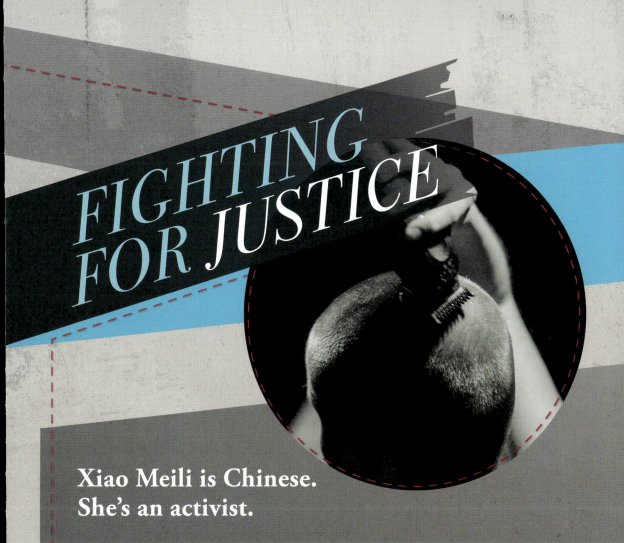

Xiao Meili is Chinese. She's an activist.

She fights for women's rights. In 2012, she was part of the "Bald Sisters." This group shaved their heads. They did this in public. They fought against unfair school admissions policies. They wanted women to be treated fairly. Their act inspired others. In 2015, Meili hosted an armpit hair contest. She questioned why armpit hair on women is ugly. She doesn't think women should have to shave their armpit hair. She said, "Men have more freedom in terms of what to do with their bodies." Women should do what they want with their body hair. They shouldn't be judged.

Glossary

activist (AK-tih-vist) a person who fights for political or social change

bobbed (BAHBD) describing a women's hairstyle in which hair is cut to chin length

bomber (BAH-muhr) a plane that drops bombs

chonmage (CHOHN-mah-GAY) a Japanese topknot hairstyle

cootie (KOO-tee) a slang term for lice

cruelty-free (KROOL-tee-FREE) free from animal testing

fashion (FAA-shuhn) any way of dressing that is favored or popular at any one time or place

lard (LAHRD) animal fat often used in cooking

pouf (POOF) hairstyle in which hair was piled up in rolled puffs

punk (PUHNK) loud, fast-moving, and aggressive form of rock music

samurai (SAA-muh-riye) member of a Japanese class of noble warriors

tinsel (TIN-suhl) thin, shiny strips of paper or plastic

trends (TRENDZ) fads or changes that are popular or common

vegan (VEE-guhn) containing no animal products

Learn More

Beaumont, Mary Richards. *The Hair Book: Care & Keeping Advice for Girls.* Middleton, WI: American Girl Publishing, 2016.

Rissman, Rebecca. *Hair-Raising Hairstyles That Make a Statement.* North Mankato, MN: Compass Point Books, 2019.

Rowlands, Caroline. *My Style & Me: Beauty Hacks, Fashion Tips, Style Projects.* London, England: Welbeck Publishing Group, 2020.

Young, Louise. Loulia Sheppard. *Timeless: Recreate the Classic Makeup and Hairstyles from 100 Years of Beauty.* Philadelphia, PA: Running Press Adult, 2025.

Index

animal products, 12, 28–29
armpit hair, 31

beauty norms, 9, 14, 31
beehives, 16–17
biases, 14, 31
big foreheads, 8–9
Black hairstyles, 14, 20
bowl cuts, 22–23

celebrity hairstyles, 12–13, 22–23
chonmage style, 10
class and status signifiers, 9–10, 12–13
coloring of hair, 6, 18, 24–25
consumer ethics, 28–30
CROWN Act (2019; California), 14
cruelty-free products, 11, 29
cultural significance, 6–7, 11, 14–15, 20

DIY projects, 21
donating hair, 30

fashion, 5
flat tops, 20
foreheads, 8–9

functionality of hairstyles, 10, 14–15, 26

gender norms, 15, 31
glitter hair, 24–25
Gumby haircut, 20

hair bias, 14, 31
hair care/styling products, 11–12, 18, 25, 28–29
hair decorations, 12–13, 16, 21, 24–25
hair length, 6, 15–18, 23, 26–27, 30–31
hairlines, 8–9
hair removal, 6, 9–10, 26, 31
hairstyles, 5–6, 10, 14–15, 17–18, 23, 30
headpieces, 8–9, 12–13

Japanese topknots, 10
Jazz Age hair, 15

laws and regulations, 14, 31
liberty spikes, 18–19
locs, 14

Marie Antoinette, 12–13
Meili, Xiao, 31
Mitchell, Holly J., 14
modern mullets, 26–27
music styles, and hair, 15, 18, 20, 23

Native hair and products, 11

punk aesthetic, 18–19

rat's nest style, 12–13
reuse/recycling of hair, 30

samurai, 10
school hair policies, 14, 31
scrunchies, 21
Simeon, Monica, 11
spikes, 18–19

trends, 4–5, 8–10, 12–13, 15–27
TurningRobe, Marina, 11

vegan products, 11, 29

wigs, 12–13, 30
women's rights, 15, 31